AUTHENTIC INDIVIDUALITY

Embracing the Refined and Defined *YOU*

Sharetta Donalson

Scripture taken from the Holy Bible, King James Version (KJV), Copyright© 1996

Brand It Beautifully™ Book Designs branditbeautifully.com

Edited by Tamika Sims of Get Write with Tamika

ISBN: 978-0-9991203-5-4

Dedication
Dreams Grow at Ms. Lynda's table

This book is dedicated to my friend and neighbor, Lynda Smith. Oh, what can two ladies accomplish while sitting at the kitchen table sipping coffee together? My answers are, a relationship and encouragement to follow dreams.

While sitting at Ms. Lynda's table, surrounded by her French Arcadian décor, I have picked up an abundance of sound advice. One evening, I expressed to her my love for writing. I even went so far as to show her the never-ending list of writing prompts that I have typed on the notepad of my cell phone. She gasped! Immediately she responded, "girl you need to get this stuff out of you". I was astonished that someone wanted to read what I had to say. I was even more shocked that she felt that my writings needed to be in print.

After both of our initial shock, we talked and laughed over another cup of coffee and moved our conversation from the kitchen table to the formal dining room. Her encouragement and empowerment continued and went on for what seemed like hours.

Her support has not wavered from that day. From advice, to encouragement, to rounding up a posse to help with my first book signing, I have never doubted her investment in my life.

Acknowledgements

I want to extend my sincere thanks to my Pastors Kevin and Leslie Wright who have poured knowledge and wisdom into my life for the last eighteen years. Thanks for your prayers, encouragement, and your pastoral labors of love.

I am also appreciative of my beta reader for this project, Alberta Miller. You never refuse to read and listen to my stories, my testimonies, and my ideas. Thanks for being an awesome sounding board.

Please pay special attention to the quotes between each chapter. They are original quotes from the women who are members of a Facebook group that I founded and currently lead called *Abba's Girls: Restored, Relentless, & Royal.* I thankful for the women who were prompted to participate in this book.

Table of Contents

Intro
Individuality on God's Terms:
Embracing the Total You

Some years ago, God impressed upon me to become a member of a local church. The teachings and worship experiences were amazing, and I began to mature like never before. The members were nice and welcoming. My children learned the Word of God on their level. My relationship with my husband was reshaping in a positive way. I had never been in such a thriving and enriching environment. I was content as long as I kept my mind on Christ. I had no question as to whether I was in the right place.

Eventually, I started to look around and compare our young family to other families. I loved my family, but we were like a motley crew in my sight. My husband and I were young parents with five children from the ages of four months to 10-years-old. We had not encountered any offensive behaviors towards us. I never saw anyone looking at us in a weird manner, but my imagination conjured up the idea that we did not measure up. God ministered to my heart by reassuring me, that we were in fact, not like any of the other families and that we were special in our own right. I learned to not covet the success and favor I assumed was prevalent in other people's lives and to embrace myself and my family as individuals without comparison.

Individuality may not be a popular subject in the Christian community or the universal church. We are a congregation. We congregate for worship services, family activities and small cell groups. Even in our group settings, we were created to be an authentic individual. God never created us to become carbon copies or clones of other people. In 1 Corinthians 12:27, we are encouraged to be individuals that are *a part* of the church. You were created to be a supplier to the body of Christ by bringing your anointing, authenticity and individuality to the table.

Your involvement in any organization should not make you blur the lines of who you are. Your authentic individuality facilitates your ministry gift and encourages your genuine service to your affiliations and to yourself. In other words, who you are is a springboard. God makes you new without wasting your uniqueness.

My least favorite quote is, "that's the way we've always done it". It leaves no room for creativity. My objective for writing this book is to empower people to live outside of societal boxes which are mostly figments of our imagination. The more we learn about ourselves, the more we gain confidence to trust our unique qualities and to not conform to mediocre uniformity.

"The next level isn't always a step up."

— Michelle Myricks of Vicksburg, MS

CHAPTER 1

Pit Experiences

We all have probably seen our share of dismal times. Before I surrendered my life to Christ and learned better, I thought Christian living was a life free of problems. Boy was I wrong! I wish I could say that you will never face another challenge in life once you decide to live for Christ. As a matter of fact, it seems as if a target is placed on your back at that time and the heat is turned up on your struggles. It was certainly not a smooth transition, but everyone's conversion is different. Your personal journey of submission surrender and obedience to God will most likely face internal and external challenges.

My husband and I have seen challenges that were more intense than we ever have, especially the year of 2018. We began the year on cloud nine financially. It seemed as if we were well on our way to begin living life more prosperous. By June, we were in dire straits. Our last two children graduated high school in May. We already had one college student and when August came, we were enrolling three.

During this time, I started having some empty nest depression. I could not handle not being the hands-on mother that I once was, and I struggled with letting my children try to make independent decisions and their own mistakes. I longed for the times they were small, and I could load them all up and have family days. During this emotional roller coaster, the everyday stressors, competitiveness on my job and maintenance of our home continued.

Life happens. It happens through our faith, prayers, fasting and any other spiritual tool that we have been equipped with. I do believe we react differently and recover more victoriously when we believe God for the best. Intense challenges might make a person rethink choosing Christianity. The Bible tells us that Job encountered so many tests, trials and tragedies until his wife told him to curse God and die, (Job 2:9).

This lifestyle is not for the faint at heart. No one is exempt. Some issues may take more time, effort and prayer to emerge from than others. The crashing, crushing, breaking, burying and pressing events of your life come to take more from you than a common cold, a fender-bender or your child's undesired progress report from school. I call these events *pit experiences.*

Pit experiences are the low, dark, dry and sunken places of life where the uncertainty of your future or your survival is depressing and unforeseeable. The inability to see the light at the end of the tunnel is suffocating and the absence of friends or familiar faces is lonely. They are the places you land in after life gives you a staggering blow. They are the places where you might question your faith in God, your worth to deserve anything from Him, or the importance of your very existence.

The pit will sometimes make you wonder if life is worth living anymore, the place where you want to die and survive at the same time. These pitfalls are designed to throw you off course. Even an inch off course will eventually become a foot. Before you know it, you will be a country mile off course of your original destination with bleak hope of returning to the right path.

Pit experiences are those that tend to strip away bits and pieces of our identity. The overwhelming blow of the pitfall makes you leave some things behind as you try to claw your way from your abyss. You're blessed to come out with your sanity without even thinking about your identity. My life has been full of pit experiences. I am sure yours has been too. Divorce, abuse, financial pitfalls, loss of employment, or deaths, anything that interrupts the normal flow of life, can be called a pit experience.

These pitfalls can be self-inflicted or caused by other people. For example, I was a teenage mother and even though I loved my child, becoming a parent at the age of 17 shifted my responsibilities and caused stressors that my immaturity was not ready for. That was a self-inflicted pitfall, even though my seven-pound bundle of joy has blessed my life tremendously.

In my last book *Forgiveness*, I talked about my history of sexual abuse. That pitfall had effects on me for a long time and even now. It was caused by another person. I only recently started recovering pieces of me that I left in that pit. After my abuse and the birth of my daughter, I stopped paying attention to the details of me. Before that, I was very meticulous about my appearance. I lost some of that. I was a neat freak who was unable to go to bed without my space being totally clutter free. I lost some of that. I loved to laugh so much so until one of my grade school teachers nicknamed me, *Grinning Jenny*. Eventually, smiles and laughs became almost as painful and sometimes not even genuine. The weight and struggle of climbing out cost me parts of my personality, values, mental status and relationships.

These pit experiences of life are most likely preceded by defining moments. It's almost as if life throws you a curve ball and says, *"If you can recover after this, then you can regain your identity, live out your purpose and be an inspiration for other people."* Joseph is an example of this. He lost so much in his betrayal to the pit. Prior to the pit, he was a dreamer, dream interpreter, favored son of his father, first born of Rachel, youngest brother, scholar, leader in training and the wearer of a multi-colored coat.

When Joseph was thrown in the pit, and subsequently sold into slavery, we see that his arrogance and naiveté starts to plummet. His story shifts. He no longer looks like the young man who had once told his brothers that he would be their leader, even though he was the youngest at the time. He no longer resembled the heir of Jacob and Rachel's union. Let's dissect the effects of his pit experience. We may locate where we are in our personal pit struggles.

One of the intentions of the pit is to strip us of our identity. When identity is lost, everything pertaining to your purpose is gone until identity can be restored. Joseph was young when he decided to share his dreams with his brothers. Maybe he didn't know that there was a process between his prophetic dreams and his promised destiny. The process has humbling power. The process has maturing power. The process has refining power. It will crush the ego of who you *think* you are and help to reestablish you for who you really are.

The first part of the process was the brothers removing Joseph's multicolored coat prior to throwing him into the pit. The brothers were obviously jealous of Joseph's coat and knew that it signified Joseph as the favored son of his father. This coat was one of a kind and Joseph could be identified by it, even if his face wasn't seen. I don't know exactly what the coat looked like, but my imagination sees the coat with vibrant and vivid colors, blinging rhinestones, sleeves to the wrists and coattails to his ankles.

It was so unique until when the brothers returned to their father with the lie of Joseph's death and the blood-drenched coat as evidence, Jacob had no choice but to believe it. In doing this, Joseph became disconnected from his father. In that time, fathers established and reinforced identity. Bloodline and legacy were important to Joseph because he had heard the history of his family and the promises that were accessible to him through Abraham. However, Jacob no longer had the opportunity to continue training and developing the young apprentice. He was now thought to be dead, removed from the father's prayers and covering. Then to top that off, while he was away, Rachel died while giving birth to their last son, Benjamin.

By that time, Joseph had been sold and relocated to a foreign land. Even though he was out of the physical pit, his pit experiences continued. He was made a slave, wrongly accused of trying to sexually take advantage of Potiphar's wife and made a prisoner in that country. The young lad who had promises of being a prince, was now treated more like a pauper. While imprisoned, he lodged with a baker and the cupbearer; however, Joseph was left alone in the prison after the cupbearer and baker received their final verdict.

After being processed for two years alone in prison, Pharaoh sends for Joseph to interpret a dream for him. Pharaoh had Joseph shaved and dressed in the clothes of Pharaoh's country. No longer is Joseph dressed in the apparel of his native country, nor is he groomed according to his tradition. This was another jab at Joseph's identity and his culture.

Joseph's betrayal by his brothers initiated the tumultuous pits of his life. He belonged to a large family, a band of brothers and a circle that shouldn't have been broken. Envy and deception soon crept in because of a young boy who couldn't keep a secret. God had given Joseph dreams of his destiny and instead of Joseph keeping his dream until a more appropriate time, he began to tell all of his heart to his brothers who were probably already envious of the first born of the favored wife Rachel. History suggests that Joseph was 17 when he was sold, so we can attribute his bragging to his age; however, the punishment that his brothers gave him did not match his offense.

Joseph was perceived to be a threat to legacy, tradition, inheritance and favor. The envy-fueled brothers figured in their minds that for Joseph to be the leader, it would be different from the norms and traditions of the older son getting the coveted blessings of the father. It's ironic that Joseph's biggest opposition came from within his family and his intimate circle. We look like Joseph to people who have limited vision and sometimes our circle acts like Joseph's brothers. When you know your identity, purpose and destiny and are surrounded by people who are unsure of theirs, it could be a recipe for a disaster. The disaster in Joseph's case was outrageous jealousy from his brothers that made them consider killing him before eventually selling him into slavery.

Be careful that you don't allow them to isolate you and make you feel unworthy. I believe that God doesn't design pits for us, but He allows them. He allows them as a part of our refining and defining processes. There were things in me that needed to die for me to start reaching for destiny. I'm sure that I'm not the only one who has battled with impurities that need to be burned out. I'll have something to work on for me until the day I die; however, what do we gain while God allows us to have these pit experiences? I have listed eight by-products of our trials and tribulations below.

1. **Humility**

2 Chronicles 20:15, "And he said, Hearken ye, all Judah and ye inhabitants of Jerusalem, and thou king Jehoshaphat, Thus saith the Lord unto you, Be not afraid nor dismayed by reason of this great multitude; for the battle is not yours, but God's."

2. **Strengthening**

2 Corinthians 12:9, "And he said unto me, My grace is sufficient for thee: for my strength is made perfect in weakness. Most gladly therefore will I rather glory in my infirmities, that the power of Christ may rest upon me."

3. **Patience**

Romans 5:3, "And not only so, but we glory in tribulations also: knowing that tribulation worketh patience."

4. **Faith-production**

Job 13:15 KJV, "Though he slay me, yet will I trust in him: but I will maintain mine own ways before him."

5. **Self-improvement**

2 Corinthians 4:17, "For our light affliction, which is but for a moment, worketh for us a far more exceeding and eternal weight of glory."

6. **Forward movement**

Hebrews 12:1 KJV, "Wherefore seeing we also are compassed about with so great a cloud of witnesses, let us lay aside every weight that so easily beset us, and let us run with patience the race that is set before us."

7. **To develop a heart for people**

1 Corinthians 12:26, "And whether one member suffer, all the members suffer with it; or one member be honored, all the members rejoice with it."

8. **Separates us to grow into our own authenticity**

Job 23:10 KJV, "But he knoweth the way that I take: when he hath tried me, I shall come forth as gold."

Favor doesn't fail.

—Veronica Utsey, Orangeburg, South Carolina

CHAPTER 2

Authentic Individuality

I didn't use Joseph's story in chapter one to encourage you to recklessly share all your dreams and aspirations nor was it shared to advocate for social isolation. The need for companionship is a fundamental human need. We need relationships. God made it that way from the very beginning when He said that it's not good that man should live alone in Genesis 2:18; however, the example of Joseph's life, was used to show you that your purpose is wrapped in your identity. It is basically impossible to fulfill your purpose apart from knowing who you are. Joseph was himself. He knew who was. He was assured of his identity and purpose through his dreams and visions and despite opposition, he never wavered from what he knew.

Although his ability to be authentic didn't save him from persecution and prison, he eventually came back to God's original plan for his life. The pit could not abort his purpose. Neither can your pits cancel your purpose, but in the lowest points in your life the essence of who you really are seems to surface to the top. You discover things about you that you had buried and forgotten. God does not forget. He knows your Divine genetic makeup. He's banking on your coming into the revelation of your Divine genetic makeup as well.

There were times when I sat in pews waiting for a preacher or prophet to lay hands on me and get a miraculous Word from God to tell me who I was and what I was called to do. I didn't know at that time that who I was, just needed to be resurfaced. Even when I started catching glimpses of my identity and my purpose, I still longed for external validation. Most people will never discover their purpose because they refuse to put in the work of self-discovery.

Discovering who you are seems simple or even insignificant. You've known yourself your whole life but trying to recapture that person or trying to have a God's eye view of you can be difficult and emotionally messy. Many people suppress their authenticity and their individuality for so many years, until they are unsure of who the real person is on the inside. Some have even compounded wearing masks or pretending to be someone else upon the self-suppression.

The decisions to suppress and wear masks are defense mechanisms to hide and conform. Who really wants to be the odd man out, the weird one, the one with the different perspective, or, the one who is labeled as controversial? I get it. I understand that it's not easy to tactfully stand alone in your own convictions with your own feelings of inadequacy; however, it is a necessary discomfort. You cannot and should not attempt to trade your authenticity for comfort and approval.

Imagine trying to fit in with the "normalcy" of life. Your parents are professionals, one is a psychiatrist and the other one is running a dental practice. You get accepted into an Ivy League Institution and realize by your sophomore year that you can't continue because you want to work on something called social media. That was Mark Zuckerberg, the founder of Facebook. I am sure that the same people that thought that he was making the biggest mistake of his life, have a wonderful Facebook page now.

Imagine converting from a seamstress to a renowned civil rights activist with one controversial and courageous act. That was Rosa Parks, an African American woman who willingly defied one of the customs of that era by not sitting at the back of the bus in order to give her seat to a Caucasian bus rider. That act along with many other brave acts of peaceful defiance and civil disobedience, made it possible for me to be able to sit wherever I want to sit on public transportation.

Imagine Noah building a gigantic boat as the towns-people looked and probably laughed and assumed, that the old drunkard had finally gone off the deep end. He was preparing for a rain that they had never seen and didn't comprehend. I wonder what the neighbors thought once they felt the first droplets of rain fall on their skin.

Imagine Jesus embracing Himself and His purpose by saying He was the Messiah while they only saw him as a carpenter. Some people never believed Him, but His identity and purpose has been passed on from generation to generation because He knew who He was.

Now the question is: *who are you?* Most people would reply to that question with alliances, accolades and accomplishments. The answer would probably go a little like this: I am Jane Doe; I am a member of the ABC organization; I graduated from ABC college; I have a degree in ABC; I am currently employed at ABC company where I manage ABC. That may be the beginning of a biographical sketch, but it's not your identity.

Your identity is the essence of who you are. In Jeremiah 1:5 KJV, the Lord said, *"Before I formed thee in the belly I knew thee."* At the point of, "in the belly," Jeremiah had performed no accomplishments. What did He know? I'm sure He knew it all because He is omnipotent. The word, "knew," is an intimate knowing. In that same verse, He explains identity, the process and the purpose. He formed Jeremiah, set him apart for consecration to fulfill the purpose and appointed him to that purpose which was to be a prophet to the nations.

Jeremiah then immediately starts to tell God of his inadequacies in the next verse. That's human nature to believe that you are not capable to achieve greatness, but God loves your imperfect individuality. He takes it, consecrates it and commissions you for greatness with it like He did Jeremiah. Your qualities, capabilities and even your weird quirks make you unique and capable of standing out from your counterparts. The way you stand out eventually propels you into your God-inspired purpose.

I was a weird young lady. If I wasn't, I certainly felt like it. Reading books, fishing and writing were my pastimes. I even enjoyed some slight carpentry work with my grandfather. I never felt like I measured with other girls who had girlish or feminine qualities because I was a tomboy. Now I fish with my husband and I can go shop for lumber for projects because of my history. Reading and writing has become another source of income. I learned to embrace me and I'm reaping great rewards because of it.

My mother even started to notice my love of reading early on. She started supporting my and my sister's literacy and imagination by ordering book series for us. On any given day, we had books coming in from Dr. Seuss, Disney, Sesame Street and the Sweet Pickles gang. The most memorable Sweet Pickles book I had was, *Me too, Iguana.* In this book, Ms. Iguana was so discontent with her identity until she started longing for the characteristics of the other animals in her neighborhood. So, she made herself a trunk out of paper like Elephant, painted herself with stripes like Zebra, made a mane like a Lion and attached feathers to herself like her friend, Goose. Her friends encouraged her to embrace her authentic individuality after Ms. Iguana desires to try and fly like her friend Stork. Iguana had become so engulfed in taking on the strengths from the other animals and trying to fit in, that she forgot her own strength. After she forsakes her purpose and becomes nearly unrecognizable, she begins to see the beauty in herself and learns to embrace her own authentic individuality.

In the natural, people get fake IDs to be able to access something that in their natural ID they have no access to, or they believe they don't deserve. Teenagers attempt to buy alcohol, get into restricted movies, or get access to social gatherings with fake IDs. Most of the time, the access that they're trying to get is unhealthy. That's exactly what we look like when we try to access perceived levels of greatness when we have no revelation of the genuine greatness that's planted within our true identity.

It is important to embrace who you are. When you are unsure or reluctant to embrace that person, then the crowd will give you an identity or you will impersonate another identity. You become what someone has told you or an impersonation. You identify with another person's vision of you or who you believe someone wants you to be. One of the worse things to see is a person that cannot break free from word curses that were spoken over their identity. Some of the deepest and darkest word curses start in the developmental stage of childhood. The negative words become a seed planted into the soul of that child, takes root and continues to grow through adulthood. Once those children become adults, they must discover who they really are, reject the word curses that were spoken and begin to live anew.

Authentic individuality is a combination of knowing who you are, feeling comfortable in being that person in any environment and at any time and fulfilling the purpose that is assigned to you despite the opposition or pit experiences. Authentic individuality is knowing that you don't have to go along to get along.

It is owning your truth, your struggles and not being afraid or ashamed to share them if need be. Another person's validation or stamp of approval isn't required but understand that sometimes accountability and apprenticeship is needed to accomplish a goal. Becoming an authentic individual does not mean that you are a lone ranger. As a matter of fact, it is knowing that you can't do it alone. You need a team. You need a tribe.

Everyone I meet tells me that I'm a strong woman but it's simply because I know who I am in Christ and I believe God's promises. I'm able to look strong even when I feel weak.

—Cheryl Stubbs, Jackson, MS

CHAPTER 3

Emotional Needs

I recently watched a video of talented actor Terry Crews on Facebook, where he shared a memory of childhood trauma he suffered as a child witness of domestic violence. He recalled the earliest memory of watching his mother getting punched in the face by his father. Even now as a strong and brawny husband and father, he was reduced to tears as he talked of his traumatic memories. He teared up as he explained having the hopes of escaping only to realize that his mother was not leaving. His mother would have him and him siblings to pack their belongings to prepare to leave, but he said, *"People in this situation feel entirely hopeless."* She could not leave.

As much as he resented his father's behavior and tried to not bring the same atmosphere into his family, he brought some of the residue from growing up in a home of domestic violence into his own home. He had control issues and residual anger, even though he never physically struck his family. He explained that he would yell at his daughter as if she was a 30-year-old man.

Crews is a successful actor; however, he explained that success is a great place to hide. Success can provide camouflage for emotional issues, but even people who are not as affluent as Hollywood stars, find places to hide and ways to mask their emotional issues. In chapter one, I explained how we lose pieces of ourselves in the pit experiences of our lives. Most of the losses that we encounter chip away at our soul, which is our mind, will and emotions. Soul scars that are not confronted leave emotional illnesses that can haunt you for a lifetime.

We lose healthy soul components and pick up fears, anxieties and uncommon desires. Those needs are heightened when you've experienced hard issues of life. Emotional needs that remain after those hard issues are usually extreme or above and beyond everyday needs. One of the needs that we normally see is that the need to be accepted can evolve into the fear of rejection or a people pleasing personality. Usually extreme emotional needs are indicative of a fragmented soul.

There is an analogy that is popular in the mental health awareness community. That analogy compares soul injuries to physical injuries. The soul injuries are called cuts and the unhealthy emotions that remain after that, are referred to as bleeding. When we are emotionally injured, we bleed on other people. Other, and sometimes innocent people, who are far removed from the original injury, get the blunt of the bleeding. Although, there are many bleeds that can spin off from emotional wounds, we will discuss only a few in this chapter.

The first one I would like to discuss is *Minimize Yourself Reflex*. I don't think that's an actual psychological term, but as a lay person that's my name for it. Some of us are so out of tune with our beauty, abilities and worth, until it's difficult to take compliments without us wedging in a flaw. For example, someone could say, "Your hair is beautiful." The knee-jerk response would be to talk about how old the style is and your need to return to the beauty salon. It is also not appropriate to talk about how much weight you need to lose when someone says you're beautiful.

My second oldest daughter was so funny when she began losing teeth in preschool. Whenever she got a compliment about how beautiful she was, she would always smile in a way that asked, "*Am I still beautiful with my teeth missing?*" It was cute for a little child and she grew out of it with some redirecting, but it is not cute or an act of modesty when adults behave the same way. I learned to accept the compliment with gratitude and when possible, find something about the person to return a compliment. Practice being comfortable with taking compliments, even appropriate compliments from people of the opposite sex. A simple thank you goes a long way.

Some people experience becoming overly aggressive after emotional wounds. This behavior can be signified by an unusual clinginess, invasiveness, or a need to always throw themselves into conversations, situations, and/or experiences. It is difficult to have meaningful relationships because this person is also easily offended and feels that they are always targeted. Some of this discontent is fueled or escalated by needs for attention and meaningful relationships that includes mutual trust. These people can sometimes think that everyone is against them or are in an unhealthy competition with them.

Another personality that is akin to the overly aggressive person, is the overly confident person. These people feel that the party does not begin until they enter the room. They are always right and despise correction and instruction. This person does not need help or encouragement to step up and be noticed. They are self-motivated, but sometimes the motives are warped by their ego. This person might need to be encouraged to scale back on their input because they are never short of opinions, philosophies, or theories. They have a false sense of security in their abilities, intellect and resources.

There are also people who suffer from the notorious lack of self-worth, self-confidence, or self-esteem. Of course, the Christian perspective to all of these is that they should be rooted in our trust in Christ and our identity in Him. We have become so well-versed at teaching children not to be haughty-minded, until we have indoctrinated some to be extremely lowly-minded. These children sometimes feel like they will never measure up.

This is very different from humility. I have heard parents tell their children that they are not God's gift to the world. Albeit, we may not be *the* gift to the world because I'd like to think that that's Christ's position; however, we are a gift *to* the world. Humility includes a balance of knowing that all that we are, and all our abilities and capabilities come from God. Recently, the administration at my job started a renovation project in my department. We met with architects and contractors several times looking at blueprints before we agreed upon the final plans. In one of the first meetings, I went in, avoided sitting at the table and grabbed a chair on the wall. I grew up in a family of carpenters, so I knew how to read a floor plan, but because of my lack of confidence, I didn't feel that I had anything valuable to contribute to the discussion.

One of the people at the table had to leave early. At that time, I felt an overwhelming prompting, which I believe was the Holy Spirit, to get up from my wallflower seat and go take a seat at the table. I moved to the table and was able to speak to what I knew. I was also able to help fellow coworkers read the blueprints because of my knowledge base.

Another group that is related to the lack of self-confidence, is the group who needs to be stroked, primed and feel a sense of validation by others to do things. These are the people who are screaming for attention and permission to be great. There is no assertion or initiative in motion here, but this person needs frequent pushing to get started and pats on the back to keep going. All of us have a need for encouragement and empowerment, but this person is stagnant unless these components are present. They are often offended if public or open kudos aren't given, especially when other people are being praised for similar accomplishments. They are usually the ones asking, "What about me?"

During my healing and self-discovery, I'm sure that I exhibited many of these behaviors. My emotional bleeds manifested more than I can probably recall. I can speak freely and with transparency on these defense mechanisms because I know I bled on people out of my brokenness, my incompleteness and my emptiness.

Those are the same reasons that some of you have bled on people. Most of the times innocent people get the anger, rage, invoked guilt, and weird clinginess when we have an emotional cut. Check your initial reaction during different situations. That does not mean that you don't need a shoulder every now and then but check the healthiness of your response.

I recently heard in my spirit, "I'm not trying to remove your emotions but I'm showing you how to control them." I was a bucket of raw, untamed, and immature emotions. My adult children tease me even to this day about my emotional instability. They didn't understand the root of the extremeness of my feelings, so they just recall crazy, funny, and sometimes scary times that they have experienced. Most of those emotions were rooted in my perception of motherly protection and my desire to shield them from harm because I had experienced times of feeling unprotected in my childhood. I knew what that felt like and I never wanted my children to even think that I wasn't their advocate; however, they were afraid to tell me at times when someone bothered them because they knew that I would show up with fury like a mother bear protecting her cubs. There was no mid-fury. My anger escalated from zero to one hundred, full throttle.

I'm excited to say that Holy Spirit has taught me differently. I'm being rewired to redirect anger and rage toward positivity. Jesus was emotional but He knew how to use those emotions to promote change, add value, and heal people. Many of the healing or restoration miracles that Jesus performed were preceded by Him being moved with compassion. His emotions created movements. The emotions were real. He allowed himself to feel them, but he channeled the emotions into positive resolutions. He is our example. We can do likewise. Allow yourself to feel. Acknowledge the emotions, then channel them wisely allowing room and time for Holy Spirit's direction.

If a person can't appreciate and respect who God has created you to be, then they don't deserve to be in your space.

—Stephanie Walker, Jackson, MS

CHAPTER 4

FOMO (Fear of Missing Out)

My oldest son introduced me to the dynamics of FOMO, which is an acronym for fear of missing out. I had never heard of it but was immediately intrigued by the reality of this in some people's lives. As I studied to write this book, I learned that the dangers of FOMO are so significant, that I decided to dedicate an entire chapter to it.

Everyone has probably experienced some sense of regret after missing an event or two. Who hasn't felt excluded when they weren't invited to the family cookout? You sat at home on the sofa and to add insult to injury, someone decides to post the pictures and videos to social media. So, you are able to watch the pictures of water balloon fights and snapshots of people biting ribs and eating corn on the cob. You watch the line dances and the outdoor family competitions. Feeling left out in this instance can be a normal emotion; however, FOMO exceeds regular regrets. It's an overwhelming anxiety that occurs when a person is thinking that others are having better and more exciting experiences than they are.

In hindsight, I realize that I had a fear of not being in relationships. I jumped from one relationship to the next or even sabotaged some relationships just to get ahead of an impending breakup. There was no exhaling or recuperation time between the relationships. There was no self- reflection or self-discovery. I didn't take the time to cultivate who I was as a person. I didn't take the time to heal after my traumatic experiences, but instead I would get out of the proverbial frying pan and then jump into the skillet; therefore, my identity and emotional welfare was always on the back burner.

The problem with that is that the more I neglected myself, the more other issues developed. I left a trail of disasters and collateral damage behind me as a result of my own emotional trauma. Now I know that there was an incomplete person inside screaming to come out on the stage of life but fears and self-rejection would shut down that emergence every time. People who suffer from FOMO have a psychological drawing to be included and involved in everything. They are determined to be in the circle, in the clique, in relationships, at socialite events and on every social media platform. This is an unhealthy attraction to the glittery things while missing out on the golden things.

Picture Eve in Paradise living her best life in the second and third chapters of Genesis. She had access to animals, the best foods, and the finest and only man on the planet. She was only excluded from one thing in the garden but could not handle that one restriction. The serpent slithered in and spoke to the part of her that feared missing out. Eve desired the scenic route in life. Then the influence she had over Adam caused him to eat from the same forbidden fruit that Eve had eaten. At that moment, they died spiritually, giving truth to the adage that curiosity kills the cat.

Her case of FOMO caused her to lose her supernatural provision, the intimate relationship they had with Father God and their provision-filled home. They were then made to labor in the fields for vegetation and to labor in childbirth to bring forth offspring. All the descendants then inherited their generational curses until Jesus came and rectified their errors.

All of this happened because Eve had FOMO and Adam followed suit. Eve already had what Satan tempted her with. He told them that they would be like God. Adam and Eve were already in the earth. They were made in the image and likeness of God, they had dominion over every living thing on earth, and they were given speak-to-create abilities just as God had. The lust for more and the fear of missing something caused them to trade dominion for powerlessness, provision for labor, and intimacy with God, for hiding in shame from Him.

What do we miss out on when we are longing to be included? As I said before, I longed for relationships. I wanted to be loved by people internally and used by God externally; however, I soon realized that sometimes the two could not coexist. Sometimes the love of people meant pleasing them and ignoring God or my own desires. I lack psychological and spiritual stamina to stand in my identity; however, I was seeking God and I was transforming into a person that didn't fit in the sinful life that I had once lived or in the life of holiness that I desired to be a part of.

I was stuck in limbo of the process of maturation by no desires of my own. The challenges of changing leaked into my relationships. One of the first relationship changes I made was in a friendship that I had for approximately 10 years. I started feeling a shift in the relationship because the things that we had in common, and the things that drew us together, became the things that I was getting deliverance from. I can remember feeling led to end the closeness of our relationship. I loved my friend, but her conversations and actions started to differ from what God was leading me to.

I could feel God calling me to a period of separation, but I wanted to hold on. One day I decided to try to negotiate with God. I wanted to go for a ride with her. It was during that trip that she decided to take the opportunity to try to teach me about tarot cards. I didn't condemn her and really didn't know how to minister to her at that time, but I did know that I wanted to be led by the Holy Spirit and not familiar spirits.

With fear and trembling, I decided to follow the leading of the Holy Spirit and separate. I still love her and hold casual conversations when I see her, but she is no longer a part of my everyday life. I do believe that if I had insisted on being in that friendship, I would have ended up in a situation that would have taken me years to rehabilitate from. I was forced to deal with my insecurity of needing to be validated by people and relationships. I know I had some recovery to do, but I didn't want to pull back those trauma memories.

Every layer of emotional flaw, immaturity and stunted growth needed to be healed. But healing for emotional and soul sickness takes time, development, and patience that I didn't feel like doing. I was busy trying to build a family, continue my education, chase a career, climb corporate ladders, and search for the American dream. I wanted to prove to myself that my past had no power over me, but it did. I had no time to heal correctly. I needed to be reset like a broken bone, but I didn't want to be immobilized long enough for the reset to take. I kept moving and ignoring me.

I also had a fear of missing out on success. Most of that fear was because I was worried about what other people would think of me because of my need for external validation. I didn't want to disappoint my parents, my children, or my younger siblings. There was no way I was allowing sexual abuse, teenage pregnancy, abortion, premature marriage and subsequent divorce, to have the final say over my life. There is a story behind most people's actions. My determination was commendable, but life continued to reroute me to the emotional baggage that I tried to evade. Like Crews, I wanted to camouflage my issues in success.

I still believe that we should pursue relationships, goals, and success but with the proper motives. Another person's validation should never drive the decisions that we make for our lives. If their approval encourages you, their disapproval can discourage you. Follow what God is doing in you and through you. He will certainly make sure that you won't miss out on HIs destiny for your life. You won't miss God-appointed connections, destinies, or possessions.

I am at age now where I am learning to walk in my purpose and to use my gifts to build confidence in other women.

—Elisha Hearon, Jackson, MS

CHAPTER 5

Pack Life

There are about three primitive instinctual behaviors that I've noticed in group settings or what I call, *pack life*. We can look at any animal life television program and see those behaviors. When we view predatory animals like lions, wolves, hyenas, we see that one of the main reasons for their group is for the effective and strategic hunt for food. When we see animals of prey like antelope, zebra, or elephant, we understand that their herding is for protection and security in sticking together. We see flocking in birds. This is mainly to reserve energy in flight. The gusts from all the wings help each bird from exhaustion.

In insects like the ant or bee, we can see the task-oriented collaboration. The larger the ant mound or beehive, the more survival tasks get accomplished. Whatever your reasoning is for your collective group, it should be for a positive outcome for you and the overall makeup of the group; however, that is not always the case. I made the correlation with animal behaviors in the last paragraph, but most of their joint efforts are instinctual. They are performing the way animals of their species have behaved for centuries. They have very little individuality, no innovation, and no self-discovery. That is also what some of our groups, clubs, and cliques start to develop into. To be apart, to belong sometimes means self-suppression, self-denial and passivity.

The disciple, Thomas, has been given a bad reputation for centuries. We have read in the Bible and saw depictions of him in movies where he would not and could not believe that Jesus had risen from the dead. We even gave Thomas a nickname and called him Doubting Thomas because of his doubt and unbelief.

True enough, Thomas may not have been listening when Jesus said several times that He would be torn down and built back up after three days; however, he was authentic. In the presence of his peers, he stated his genuine thoughts that there was no natural way that Jesus could have risen after being in the tomb for three days. How many times have you suppressed your real thoughts and fresh ideas because you thought the crowd was smarter or more experienced than you?

How many times have you participated in something that you really didn't want to because you wanted to remain in good graces with the crowd? How many times have you lied and said that you had no questions or comments because you thought your peers would not understand you? It is okay to be in a group, but your authenticity should not belong to that group. Peers sometimes bring pressures. Our kids are not the only ones who experience peer pressure; although, they are more likely to be influenced by peers than adults. We fear standing in our own beliefs because packs sometimes turn cannibalistic where members of the group defy nature, turn on each other and feed off each other because of misunderstood and envied differences.

I watched the movie *The Help*. There was a group of Caucasian socialites that basically tried to hold each member to a standard of superiority over the African American maids. The members of the group had to basically treat the maids as second-class citizens in order to belong. To be empathetic or loving to the maids would result in the cannibalistic behavior that I spoke of. The reputation and social status of that exiled member would be basically eaten alive. As a result, that, "negro-loving," socialite would be exiled and black-balled. The group was fueled by copycatting, false senses of security and the needy behavior of up and coming socialites to belong.

I am a nurse by trade. There is a true phenomenon described as, "Nurses eat their young." This is another example of cannibalistic behavior where younger and less experienced nurses are *eaten* or treated as inferior to the older, more experienced nurses. Basically, the younger nurse is shunned for everything they don't know, or for every mistake that they make instead of being mentored by the more experienced nurse.

All nurses do not behave in this manner. More are starting to understand that withholding information and highlighting every mistake is a form of bullying that should not exist in the professional peer group, especially one that has a reputation of helping others and preserving lives. I have seen a shift in the mindset happen in the nursing communities that I have been a part of for the last 20 years. Basically, the intimidation of the older, more experienced nurses was promoted by fear that the younger, more innovative and energetic nurse would get the attention, raises, and promotions; therefore, cannibalism was a form of oppression.

Cannibalism is wrong and is a form a bullying that should not exist in any of our settings, but we can learn a lot from the other pack behaviors and how they can positively be in operation in our groups. We can take the savage and instinctual behaviors of animals and show how they can healthily be present in our group. For example: We talked about the lion packs. We understand that one of the reasons that the lion congregates in packs is for a quick, effective and strategic hunt. We should do the same things. Goals, purpose, and accomplishments should be prey to our groups. We should do that together as a collaborative team.

One of my favorite meanings for team is **T**ogether **E**veryone **A**chieves **M**ore. Collaboration is key. We cannot be insecure and attempt to hog every step of our processes because we have a psychological need to receive all the kudos from people. We can accomplish so much more together instead of trying to be lone rangers. Lone rangers sometimes never get anything accomplished or are delayed in their accomplishments because they attempt to do everything, but master nothing. The lioness is a master of the hunt for the pack. She knows her role that is important for the survival of the whole pack.

The lion represents the pack behavior that hunts and prey, now let's talk about the pack behavior that protects. Everyone needs safety in their groups. We should cover each other just as the herding animals the zebra, elephants and antelopes. I noticed some of the elephant herds will not leave the younger more vulnerable calves alone. They are protective and they help to cover the vulnerabilities of their peers. You hardly ever see these animals isolated, alone and easily exposed to be picked off by the enemy. They protect each other. Of course, they know that most of the time they can't fight the predators off in a one-on-one combat, but they understand the herding behavior is one of their best defenses.

I love to listen to old stories. I can remember hearing that in decades past when couples were having marital problems, people would pray for them, cook food and bring it to their house, keep their children, and be an overall support to help the couple survive the rough marital patch and hopefully help the marriage survive. In other words, friends, neighbors, and family would come in to help protect the survival of the family unit. They knew that the ultimate decision rested on the husband and wife, but they helped to provide protection by assisting with other needs so that the couple could give more attention to what was broken or vulnerable in the marriage.

Oftentimes, we don't take the opportunity to help cover and protect other people. Sometimes covering and protecting also means reporting to proper people as well. Remember, I said that I'm a nurse. I worked HIV care for a while and absolutely enjoyed it. My job was to protect the privacy of my patient's health while delivering quality care. Even though their privacy is protected by law, if I encountered a newly diagnosed patient, I had to disclose that to the local health department.

So, I do understand that disclosure to the proper officials is necessary in some cases, but intentional character assassination is never necessary. Don't go to social media and camouflage exposing a person's business inside a prayer request by saying, *"Everyone pray for my friend Elizabeth, she's going through tough times in her marriage."* That is inappropriate and does not protect or cover, but sometimes invites gossip and attention from people who do not have Elizabeth's best interest at heart.

We can also benefit from the flocking behavior of birds. So many times, we hear the cliché, *"Birds of a feather flock together."* It's usually said by parents as a warning to their children to choose their friends wisely; however, there is a positive reasoning for the flocking that can be used in our everyday life. We can collaborate and move in unison on projects to avoid over-exertion of one person. Wind gusts from the wings help to preserve the energy of each bird. A canoe team understands this concept. They must all paddle in unison and at a synchronized cadence. The team that has mastered teamwork, wins medals. Your ability to work well with others will also help you to win in life.

The last behavior was likened to that of the ant and bee. These people are great support people. They might not be aggressive in the hunt, but they are able to pool resources together to make sure the opportunities and tasks are accomplished. These are your administrative people. If you have ever seen a line of ants traveling back to their mound carrying food that is double or triple their size, you know what I mean. The worker might not have a dominant or leadership personality, but the group needs them. Sometimes these are the people who have connections, who know where to get resources from, and who keep their ears to the ground to hear information that may help the group accomplish goals. The Bible says in *Psalms 6:6-8 ESV, "Go to the ant, O sluggard; consider her ways, and be wise. Without having any chief, officer, or ruler, she prepares her bread in summer and gathers her food in harvest."* The ants do not only prepare for today, but in their administrative way, they continue to look to their future for longevity and the posterity of their population.

Each of the animal groups, herds, and collaborative species come together for their own purposes. These groups possess their own personality and their own instinctive rules or ways of getting things done. We should possess some of the personalities of animal groups in our group and individually in some part, even though one personality will be dominant over the others. How does your group operate? What's the personality of your group? Why are you there? Have you experienced some of the herding practices in your group? Are you in the correct group? I heard someone say that if you're the smartest person in your group, maybe you're in the wrong group. Now would be a great time to evaluate the efficacy of your tribe.

I know just what I want! I know just who I am!

—Fredricka Cross, Jackson, MS

CHAPTER 6

Desire More

One of my favorite movies gives the depiction of a coming of age Prince who decides that he's ready for marriage. The young, handsome fellow was the only son and had been groomed for the royal spotlight since birth. He was betrothed to a young princess who had been groomed to be his wife since her birth. She basically had no identity other than to become the wife of the Prince. This did not appeal to the Prince. In his quest to fulfill his own individuality and to seek a bride who was authentic, he leaves his kingdom and his family and travels halfway across the world in search of a woman who was assured of her own individuality and that could genuinely love him for the man he was aside from his royalty.

He desired more than a woman who didn't know her own likes and dislikes but knew all of his only because she was programmed to please him. He didn't want just a warm body; he wanted a partner who really loved him. He decided to leave the comfort of the kingdom to pursue true love. He desired more. Desiring more is a balancing act between contentment and complacency. Contentment is a state of being happy, thankful, and satisfied with your present circumstances while remaining open-minded for improvement. Complacency is a satisfaction with no desire for better or more.

After my life got railroaded by sexual abuse, I became a different person. I felt like the trauma had literally re-programmed my personality. My natural life had been destroyed by unnatural circumstances. It took a rebirth in Christ for me to unpack all my issues and return to God's original design for my life. The more I learned about myself, the more I desired to learn. I desired more.

Abraham desired more. In Genesis 11, the history of Abraham begins with him in the place of his birth, Ur of the Chaldeans. After Abraham's brother, Haran, dies in Ur, Abraham's father, Terah, decides to journey towards Canaan. Terah moved and took his entire family with him including Haran's son Lot, Abraham, and Sarah. They traveled to a country of Haran that they probably named after Abraham's deceased brother. Abraham's father died in Haran and never got to the Promised Land.

In the next chapter, we see God instructing Abraham to leave his company and follow his guidance to a place that He would show Abraham as he travels. Abraham's obedience meant that he desired more and wanted to fulfill his purpose in life. Abraham had to move if he wanted the promises of God. I am sure that Abraham loved the people and place of Haran. After all, it was named after his deceased brother. We also love our friends and families. We need our churches. We enjoy the fellowship in our clubs and organizations; however, sometimes elevation comes after separation.

Before you find rocks to stone me with or throw your book across the room because I mentioned family and church, let me explain. I am not advocating anyone leaving their family. I am simply saying, don't be restricted by yours. Don't miss your opportunities or deny your gifts and talents because there's not an example of it in your family. You may be the trendsetter or the one who is changing the trajectory of your bloodline. That's exactly what Abraham did. He established a bloodline of faith.

Some churches are your training grounds for greater. As a young girl growing up in my childhood church, I learned a lot. I left at 17 on my own account, but while I was there, I learned Biblical stories, how to represent my church at different meetings and conferences, and overall church etiquette, i.e. avoid walking in service, no chewing gum, no talking and no walking during prayer. That was part of my foundation and training. Some areas of elevation require you to move. Great leaders will willingly train you, equip you and send you out as they are led by the Holy Spirit. However, our unwillingness to move can stunt our spiritual growth and delay our coming of age naturally and spiritually. Notice the separation noted below:

Acts 13

1.	Now there was in the church that was at Antioch certain prophets and teachers; as Barnabas, and Simeon that was called Niger, and Lucius of Cyrene, and Manaen, which had been brought up with Herod the tetrarch, and Saul.
2.	As they ministered to the Lord, and fasted, the Holy Ghost said, Separate me Barnabas and Saul for the work whereunto I have called them.

3. And when they had fasted and prayed, and laid their hands on them, they sent them away.

God is a progressive God. He desires that we grow and expand to continue to spread out to others. He also wants a relationship with us where He is first place and preeminent, where we consult Him first and obey Him despite any earthly opposition or opinions. We must quiet our affiliations to hear the sincere heart of God. Your identity and purpose will somehow rise to the top like rich cream if you live a life of progression. In the book of Esther, we see a royal couple whose real individual identities comes through under pressure.

After King Ahasuerus puts his wife out, he, along with his staff, begin to search for another. Hadassah, a young Hebrew girl whose Persian name was Esther, became a candidate to become the new queen. On the advice of her Cousin Mordecai, she kept her identity a secret and only used her Persian name, Esther. The King hired an assistant named Haman who came with an ulterior motive to annihilate the Jews.

In order to save her people, Esther decides to reveal herself to her husband as the Hebrew Hadassah. She comes unannounced before her husband and the princes of the land and commits a crime greater than the wife before her, who would not come when she was called. At this moment, the king had to cover and protect Hadassah as her husband. He eventually executed Haman and issued a decree to protect the Jews and to allow them to protect themselves.

I told that story just to show you how the pressures of life and different situations will stretch you to the point where the real you come forth. The king and Esther both desired more. Esther desired to save her people. The king desired to keep his wife and to save her people. Ahasuerus was Esther's king, but he showed himself to be Hadassah's husband. When you want your life to have purpose, a defining moment will eventually happen that will catapult you from your comfort zone and right back into your real identity and a God-designed outcome.

Jesus is calling us to come forth out of the tombs! He wants to remove our grave clothes of shame, fear, and self-rejection in order to resurrect newness of life within us.

—StepieJ, Jackson, MS

CHAPTER 7

Breakout Season

E sther had to have been different from the other young ladies in the harem. Her differences drew the attention and love of the King. Isn't it amazing how the different girl was the very girl that God used to bring relief to her people? Your difference peaks interests. Your authenticity and individuality also peak interests. Today marks your breakout. Break out of what, you may ask? This is your time to break out of what people think, to God's design for your life. The most powerful times of my life have been when I dared to be me and refused to be caged and limited by the opinions of other people. The times when I listened to the heart of God and decided that I was going to dance to His heartbeat instead of the drumbeat of other people have been the most rewarding. It took courage. It took stamina. You must make an informed and tenacious decision to not dim down, or dumb down, to make anyone feel comfortable with who you are and what God has called you to do.

One of the most quoted lines from Shakespeare's Hamlet is, *"To thine own self be true."* This quote could have several meanings, but for the sake of this book, we want to focus on you living out your authenticity and your truth if only for the primary reason of self-fulfillment and liberty. We have worn masks for other people. We have tried to fit in but felt incompatible like a square peg trying to conform to a circular opening. We have considered everyone's feelings but have neglected the very purpose that God has for our lives because it's connected to the part of you that you refuse to confront. Your truth sets you free but keeps you free perpetually.

The title of this chapter paints a picture in my mind of a big, angry bull, bucking behind the constraints of the gate just prior to being turned loose at a rodeo. He's boxed inside of a cage. He despises the cage and simply wants to be left alone. Nothing around him looks like the green pastures that he would probably rather be grazing in. The stadium is noisy and to add to that someone has mounted his back. When the gates finally open, he charges forth with all his might bucking even more trying to find an exit from the mayhem. He is violent and dramatic. We don't have to wait until we are as frustrated and overwhelmed by a restrained life as the bull before we embrace our identity. We don't have to wait until our true self is buried so deeply by our identity crises until it takes a miracle for us to dig our way out of it and find out who we truly are. You can start today by stripping the layers of self-denial away.

The following exchanges may be beneficial to help you to uncover secret struggles with accepting and maintaining your personal God-ordained greatness.

I. Silence the voice of inferiority. You are doing yourself and no one else any favors by feeling, thinking, or behaving as if you are inferior to anyone. Kill the thought that you don't measure up to other people. They are really not the example that you're trying to be. Jesus is your example. Humans have flaws. Your flaw just may differ from the person that you believe has it all together. You can't build your confidence by continually watching people. Watch God. Appreciate how far He's brought you. It ok to see people's accomplishments and admire them, but it's not okay to see their accomplishments and shrink down to the point where you neglect what God is trying to do in you and through you. Read through your Bible and you will see how God used flawed people to accomplish great things. Just add yourself to the roster of flawed people that will accomplish many things under the leading of the Holy Spirit.

Exchange inferiority for strength. You are stronger than you think. Know that when you feel weak in an area of your confidence, the joy of the Lord is your strength as recorded in Nehemiah 8:10. It takes strength to fight your inner critic. It takes strength to fight what you think others are thinking about you. It takes strength to pursue any goal when you simply don't think you deserve it. Please understand that you are an heir of God and a joint heir with Christ, (Romans 8:17). You don't qualify for the blessings and favor because of yourself, but because of your Divine heritage. Strengthen your faith by those facts. You are not enough standing alone. In Christ, you are more than a conqueror. Strengthen up and conquer that sense of inferiority.

II. Silence Your Desperation to Compromise
In Daniel chapter 3, we see three young Hebrew boys, Shadrach, Meshach and Abednego, who refused to bow to

an idol as the powerful King commanded. They knew that to stand their ground could possibly mean death. They refused to compromise their faith and as a result when they were sentenced to be burned alive, Jesus himself showed up to rescue them. The story of the three Hebrew boys was not written for our entertainment. It was written to increase our hope, edify us, and give a jolt to our faith in a God that is the same now as He was then.

When it seems like you're always the last one chosen to be on the team, the pressure to compromise becomes evident. Do not let what acceptance does for your psyche excite you to the point where you forfeit the plans and purposes of God for your life. Be steadfast and immovable in God. When you compromise, it is very detectable to the people who you are compromising for. It isn't authentic. Be uncompromisingly authentic. You'll stand out gracefully instead of sticking out like a sore thumb.

Embrace your values. The first step in embracing your core values is to define them. What things do you consider when you want to become a part of certain groups, organizations, or relationships? No one will probably encompass everything you believe or hold dear, but there are some values that are top of the line for me. For example, if I am in a relationship, I must have liberty to be who I am and walk in my truth. I am unwilling to compromise on that. On my job, I must have room for error without fear of termination being thrown at me on every mistake. Family is important to me. I must have time for my husband and children. When I'm about to engage in a new endeavor or already engaged in something, I must weigh the time that it will take away from my home. I have those discussions with my husband.

I must always assure him and my children that they are a priority in my life no matter how golden an opportunity may seem. Everything that glitters ain't gold, as the old saying goes. Your acknowledgement of your values helps to escort you into what would really be golden in your life. I have learned not to chase glitter or shiny things because the golden things are what matter. Make a list of what matters most to you not to engage in political or social arguments or debates, but to make conscious decisions on what you can or cannot align yourself with. Be known for the things you do agree with instead of highlighting the things you don't. You will have a stronger and more solid relationship when you do.

III. Silence Your Temptation to Compare Comparison is the thief of joy is a popular quote that partially summarizes what comparing yourself to others can do to you. Comparison steals joy, peace, focus, and the sense of contentment in your abilities and accomplishments. We usually compare ourselves to others when we think we aren't doing enough. Somehow, we think that other people have it all together and we don't have as much to offer. Struggles are common to us all.

The people that we compare ourselves to have issues and struggles just as we do. We just paint a false representation of their lives in our heads. Even if they have everything together, comparison does not profit us or our purpose at all. Stop overthinking your steps and just move forward. Other people should not be the gauge by which you measure yourself. You have a Divine lane that you have been ordained to operate in. Find that lane because that's where your anointing is. Even if others are speeding past you, stay focused in the lane of your anointing and your grace.

Embrace Your Unique Abilities and Momentum. Most people have goals and aspirations, gifts and callings, and anointing and abilities. Our goal should be to customize and direct all those positive attributes to accomplish something in the Kingdom of God. We are servants, serving others with our God-given capabilities. There should be no competition and comparison when it comes to taking care of God's people. Embrace what you bring to the table to help serve people. God gives us gifts and we return the favor by giving Him results. Stay on your destined pace.

Don't be like Abraham and Sarah who were so eager to have a child that Ishmael was born as a result. When their child of promise, Isaac, finally began to grow, Ishmael began to mock the promise. Don't allow your destiny to be mocked by premature projects that you create because you believe God isn't efficient. Not only is God efficient, but the works that He's doing in you are effective. Remember the promises of God are yes and Amen. You won't have to mimic someone else to be a success in Christ.

IV. Silence Your Fear of Rejection. The fear of rejection is apprehension caused by thinking that you will not be accepted or approved because of your looks, abilities, or socioeconomic status. Fears are debilitating and the fear of rejection is no different. You limit your options when you consider other people's opinions prior to making any moves towards your purpose. Some of the things that you are called to do may not please people. God can restore relationships. I knew when I wrote my first book and told my testimony of sexual abuse that I might experience some rejection. I was certainly apprehensive when I considered all of the people that I stood a chance of losing, but I was reminded of this Scripture: *Mark 10:29-30, "And Jesus answered and said, Verily I say unto you, There is no man that hath left house, or brethren, or sisters, or father, or mother, or wife, or children, or lands, for my sake, and the gospel's. But he shall receive an hundredfold now in this time, houses, and brethren, and sisters, and mothers, and children, and lands with persecutions; and in the world to come eternal life."*

Don't let your fears stall you, but instead allow them to propel you. When I was a little girl, we used to listen to a gospel quartet group sing this song, "I'll Go if I Have to Go by Myself." Some roads you will travel with only you and your Creator. Go the distance with Him understanding that your primary objective is to be obedient unto Him by being light and salt in this world.

Embrace Your Worth. The fear of rejection undermines your worth and talents. Don't be intimidated by the word, "no." Sometimes they shield us from impending doom. Don't worry if you don't get an invitation. Protection sometimes comes disguised as rejection. We can't spend our lives preoccupied with peeping through windows to see their lives either. You are equipped to handle your life with or without the crowd. You are perfectly flawed. Your perfection is in Christ and He helps with all flaws, imperfections, and inconsistencies. You cannot afford to seek the approval of other people when you are moving in obedience to God with the vision that He has for your life.

Your worth is definitely not calculated by people's opinions of you. You don't have a point to prove or dis-prove. God vindicates and validates. We want His seal of approval in all that we do. This does not mean you reject Godly counsel, mentorship, direction, or correction from reputable sources. I do believe in accountability partnering and skilled coaching that helps to instruct and equip. Pray for and seek the ones that God will have you to learn from. Authentic people need authentic leadership that's willing to pour into you with hopes of you succeeding. You are worth having someone in your life to add to what God is doing without trying to muzzle it.

As you develop relationships, unapologetically allow people to make informed decisions on whether they can handle being in a relationship with the authentic and awak-ened version of you. Start embracing who you are and all your weird quirks not because you are so great, but the God who created you is. Break free from your people pleasing and people appeasing. Take a stand to value the quality of relationships over the quantity, but more importantly, value you. *"Let me be great,"* is a popular saying now that implies someone else has power over whether you will be great or not. You are already great and no one's permission is required to make you that way. You were born that way. The disconnect may just be between you being great and you accepting your greatness as fact.

You share DNA with some of your biggest supporters and greatest critics! Don't be moved! What did God say though?

—Sharetta Donalson, author

CHAPTER 8

Healthy Connections

Authentic and Divine connections are important in helping to promote, establish and sustain your individuality. You will need to discover what those relationships will actually look like for you. I envision my authentic relationships to be pressure-free. There's no pressure to conform to another person's likes and dislikes. There's no pressure to agree with their every philosophy. There's no pressure to contact that friend daily and there is no pressure to avoid any other friendships. As a matter of fact, we would respect each other's boundaries, relationships, beliefs and time, even in the areas that I'm not necessarily included.

You may notice relational changes as you go through and emerge from your breakout season. It's bound to happen. Your mindset is transforming, your motives are getting focused, and your maturity is developing. This does not mean that you have finally arrived at a place of perfection or superiority. It may simply mean that the things you had in common, are no longer common or no longer the driving force for the relationships. This shift may be painful to acknowledge, but the goal is for your good, not for evil, and to give you an expected end, (Jeremiah 29:11).

One of the most vulnerable and disappointing places you can find yourself, is a place where you feel deserted.

That's the place where you notice that all the people who started out with you are no longer there. This is the place where you thought that people would be there forever only to realize that the people who you thought had your back have backed away. We despise individuality for these reasons.

This place can be lonely and make you self-reflect. I know one of the first reactions would be to check yourself to see if you've done something wrong. Don't internalize it. Something has shifted the relationships. Please understand that every connection you make will not last the duration of your lifespan. We grow apart and sometimes outgrow the conditions by which our relationships were established in the beginning. This is a normal part of life.

When Joseph was alive and in Egypt during the famine, the children of Israel were welcome to live there. After Joseph died and the old Pharaoh died and a new Pharaoh came into power, the children of Israel became enslaved. The relationship with Israel and Egypt shifted and outgrew the original purpose of why they initially became connected. As a result, God commissioned Moses to go and demand the Israelites freedom and to assist them in transitioning from bondage through the wilderness to the Promised Land.

Although the Israelites were eventually freed, Pharaoh refused to comply to a peaceful resolution. Instead, as he tried to battle against the arm of the Lord, the Israelites release was pressured through pestilences, plagues, and premature death in which the children of Israel were Divinely protected. Through it all, Pharaoh lost his firstborn son, his army and his standing as god on earth to his citizens.

Don't be like Pharaoh. When people desire to be released from your life, please allow them to do so peacefully and as painless as possible. I do believe in trying to hold marriages and other family relationships together if possible, but we can't hold people hostage to our relationships if they have no desire to be there. We can't hold people hostage to our emotions and insecurities. It is unhealthy to try to keep someone who doesn't desire to be kept. This will not be profitable to either party.

Authentic people need authentic and healthy relationships. Authentic and healthy relationships are not established on intimidation, manipulation and domination. In healthy relationships, there should be mutual openness to differences, open communication and an openness to be vulnerable. Most relationships that function outside of those realms of openness often possess some level of oppression.

Oppression is evident when we try to force people to conform to a certain system without a reasonable, humane, or otherwise justifiable foundations. Romans 12:2 KJV says, *"And be not conformed to this world, but be ye transformed by the renewing of your mind that you may prove what is that good, and acceptable, and perfect, will of God."* The Amplified translation is a little more extensive in its take on Romans 12:2, see below:

Romans 12:2 AMP, *"And do not be conformed to this world [any longer with it superficial values and customs], but be transformed and progressively changed {as you mature spiritually] by the renewing of your mind [focusing on godly values and ethical attitudes], so that you may prove [for yourselves] what the will of God is, that which is good and acceptable and perfect [in His plan and purpose for you}."*

The choices are to be conformed to the world's system or be transformed by the will and by the power of God. He gives us freedom under that auspice to make decisions and to live in a world peacefully without having to conform in order to seem righteous. We are different. And that's ok. Even within Christianity, we are different. In our family, we are different. We must be open to those differences in other people if we desire to have authentic relationships with them. We can't demand people to like what we like, dress how we dress, and live how we think they should live.

I dare to say that sometimes Christians give people the hardest times with this. We have a boxed-in view of what Christianity should look like and we reject people who don't necessarily fit into those boxes. Even if we don't reject them, we fail to embrace them. The world needs love and we are love agents. Let's focus on delivering the love and allow the Holy Spirit to focus on the changes, if any, that people need to make in their lives. Honestly, sometimes love provokes change because your love becomes Jesus personified.

Being open to people's differences and showing your authenticity, can also make a way for you to have open communication. Communication is at least a two-way dialogue. You must be present and interactive with people that you desire to communicate with. Open communication is an upgrade because it includes trust, truth and transparency. Open communication can be fearful and is not something that I expect to happen with someone that I am not expecting to have a deep relationship with. We may be open with people who we have decided to include into our lives on a more intimate level, for instance, parents, prayer partners, accountability partners, counselors, close friends, Pastors, and of course, spouses.

I realized one day that I had had many superficial conversations with my husband but failed to openly communicate with him on several issues. Most reasons that we try to hide or just fail to talk about certain issues is the fear of judgement, fear of change, and the fear of abandonment. So open communication then makes us open to being vulnerable.

I do not know anyone who is just anxious and excited about being vulnerable. Most people want to be in control and composed. Being vulnerable can deepen your relationships with people and with God. I am becoming more vulnerable with age. As a younger person, I had points to prove. I had to prove my strength and abilities. My place of vulnerability is now that I really wasn't that strong alone, I had Divine help in the power of God. In our brokenness with God, we invite Him to be the person that we need, we depend on and that we can't make it without. Most of the times, we can't arrive at a place of authentic vulnerability with people if we have not surrendered to God.

I tell Him my secrets, likes and dislikes. I tell Him what I struggle with and what I need His intervention on. Does He already know all things? Of course, He does; however, I am being authentic and open with Him, displaying my vulnerability and not trying to hide from an all-knowing God. I do the same in my marriage. I include my husband in on things that I struggle with, things that are tempting, or things that could be a potential pitfall if left a secret. One day, I received a ten-dollar electronic cash gift for our ministry from a gentleman that my husband and I both know. I made sure that I immediately reported that to my husband. There was no ill intent in the gift, but I know how small things can blow up. I was in a vulnerable space of disclosure to him because I value our relationship.

My co-pastor, Leslie Wright, always reminds us that the enemy thrives in anonymity. Shedding light on situations through openness can foster healing and keep straight-forwardness and integrity in relationships. We started this chapter talking about the enslavement of the children of Israel who ended up in slavery due to a lack of straightforwardness and integrity. I am sure that none of the openness that I mentioned was maintained in their relationship with Egypt. The children of Israel basically had no choice in how they ended up in a twisted relationship with Egypt.

They started on good terms, but Egypt switched the dynamics of the relationship midway because they were jealous of the prosperity of Israel. Sometimes the key to not entering these relationships is knowing your role and the overall goal for the relationship. Please learn who you are before you enter relationships especially ones that you want to be long-lasting like marriages. If you are wearing a mask, the person you enter relationship with is in a relationship with a façade. Simply put, you are intentionally or unintentionally in relationship under false pretenses. If the relationship lasts and you want to prosper in your truth, you will have to become the authentic you and de-program the other party to get to know the real you. Odds are, if you were not genuine, you have attracted someone who wasn't either.

Make sure that you are an original representation of you. Your originality inspires others.

—Tameka Clincy-Champion, Canton, MS

CHAPTER 9

Real Recognizes Real

In our world of information and technology, it's easy to access things on the internet and have millions of resources in one engine search. Certifications, licensure and other credentials can also be printed within seconds after pressing the enter button. There's also a new term, *catfishing*, where a person that you may be communicating with online has shown a picture and given a name that is not really them. How do we know what people are presenting to us is truthful and accurate? Aside from the technological advances, we hear news of deception in many arenas of our world including politics, corporate America and even the church. This high-level and widespread deception has made it hard for people to trust each other.

Most of the times you can't know the intent and motives of every person's heart that comes into your life. Starting with your self-awareness does help. Examining your own motives and performing heart checks on a regular basis is important to your emotional health and self-awareness. I can't say that I have totally arrived in my emotional well-being. I have gained friends and lost them, but I present the real person that I am in this stage of my emotional development. I just realized that in my authenticity, that my "no's," are a little sharp. Since loving kindness is a fruit of the Holy Spirit, I must allow that fruit to continue to grow more in me. We are all in the process of recognizing and living out the realness in ourselves.

We are removing layers of masks and pretentious behaviors as we go and as we grow. Not only are we removing, but we are also uncovering the core of who we are. As a member of the Christian faith community, I don't believe we give people enough time, space and grace to grow into their realness and into their authenticity. We cast wounded people away and label them as being involved in heathenism, witchcraft, demonology and other occult activities without accessing the very Holy Spirit who promised to show us all things in the situation. How quickly we forget that we were once unsure and searching for authenticity in our lives and God forbid that we should hit a snag and end up there again.

Each one of us needs a level of truth, authenticity, and stability in our lives. The truth of the matter is, that we cannot put the value and weight of that need on another human being. It is unfair to do so. God is the constant and truth in my life. Most people are giving out only what they are capable of giving out at the current juncture in their lives. Just as you present your current self to other people and give people the option to accept that or not, we must choose what we are willing to deal with or discern what God is assigning us to deal with in the moment.

Understanding this has set me free from being the perpetual victim. I understand that in most cases the level of authenticity and genuineness that I expected and didn't receive was unrealistic because the person wasn't capable of giving it. Honestly, I have been incapable of reciprocating people's expectations as well.

My mother had an old alarm clock when I was younger. It was the kind that she had to wind up in the back so that it could alarm really loud and forceful at the appointed time. One day I decided to play with that clock while she wasn't watching. I wound it up until I broke the knob off. I panicked because I knew I shouldn't have been in her room in the first place. So, I set it back down and went on about my day as if I did nothing. When she found the clock that night, she questioned everyone. I wouldn't fess up. Everyone got in trouble because I refused to be truthful. Sometimes our attempt at self-preservation trumps the truth and the real person continues to get suffocated by our inability to cope, communicate and conquer the challenges.

One of the statements that we used during the 80s and 90s hip hop era was, *"real recognize real."* A person was not considered real if there was any deception, disloyalty, or divided affections noted within them. *Urban Dictionary* defines real recognizes real as an idiom of the hip-hop culture used to refer to the tendency or ability for real individuals to identify, connect with, or otherwise respect other real individuals. Real here means authentic and genuine as much as possible.

This includes appreciating the quality of genuine connections over the quantity. Genuine people will be drawn to you and genuine relationships can flourish better. As you nurture those genuine relationships, the more they will grow and outgrow the weedy relationships in your life. People that are not attracted to your genuine authenticity will not stay around long.

One of the things that I am in the process of learning in my journey is to see the realness in people is to acknowledge the yellow or red flags. The yellow flags of course are encouraging me to slow down. When I sense these, obviously I'm doing too much, too fast. At which time, I might have to slow down for a while. Sometimes our desperate desire for business partners, friends and spouses can have us head over heels while the other person is still trying to figure you out. Acknowledge the yellow flags and slow down. Having an objective voice of reason might be wise at that time. Just recently, I was asked very bluntly by a person that I was in partnership with, *"What are your intentions?"* Although, I had no ill intentions in our relationship, I realized after a more in-depth conversation, that we were not compatible for the ventures that we were attempting to do. That didn't make either of us bad people. Now, we were both empowered to maturely acknowledge our red flags.

Communicate truthfully with people. The Bible says in Matthew 5:37 to let your no be no and your yay be yay. Sometimes your answers may be disappointing, but at least they're authentic. Communicate your boundaries. You may not be the popular person then, but when people are searching for truth, they will search for you. When people are looking for what you stand for, they will find you.

You can't recognize the authenticity in other people, if you continue to hide who you are. Present your authentic and consistent self. I am vocal and strong in my convictions. Then there are times when I like the stillness and tranquility. I have a passionate love for people, but I never present myself as someone who is extremely extroverted. That would be unfair to the person who expected more out of me than I can give. After an hour or so, I'm ready to get home to my sofa. I've acknowledged and embraced that about me. Trying to force more sometimes becomes awkward.

There is a tribe of people that are attracted to you. Although, you may have some differences, your similarities will outweigh them. They will recognize your real qualities and your real value without you having to change your individuality that you possess. There is another hip-hop idiom that said, "*You ain't gotta lie to kick it.*" In other words, you don't have to pretend to be someone you're not just to be accepted. If you are out of sync with the tribe that you are in and you have tried to do what others are doing because you want to belong, you are doing the world a disservice in drowning out the real you. Let the real you stand up. I guarantee you this, someone will see you and be drawn to the quirks and the perks that are attached to being in your presence.

Self-Reflection is a humbling experience when you can accept why you do, say, and think the way you do.

—Jacqueline Thompson, Charlotte, NC by way of Chicago, IL

CHAPTER 10

Plan A: You are ENOUGH

ooking back on my pre-teen years of the jheri curl hair and acne-ridden face little timid person, I never thought that I would be writing a book about this subject, especially this chapter. I was a skinny tomboy that had been called Olive Oyl, long-legged, clumsy, and lanky, and a wild deer that was silly and couldn't seem to grow up. It amazes me how I remembered those phrases and how long the insults stayed with me. To add to that, my battle with sexual abuse, teenage motherhood and every unwise decision I ever made, kept me thinking that I needed to prove something to onlookers. I always wanted to show that I can still make it, no matter what happened.

When you consider your tragedies, traumas, trials, tribulations and even your triumphs. It's easy to wonder what life would've been like had they not occurred. I'm guilty of letting my mind drift in that direction as well. How would I have been had I not been molested, rejected, unprotected and misunderstood? I have even thought about things that I didn't experience and wondered how I would be if I had experienced them.

For example, my mother's father died when she was 10 years old. Obviously, that means I never had a chance to meet him, but I heard stories of what an awesome and doting father he was to her. I made him out to be an imaginary hero that I desired to save the day. In some of my lowest times, I longed for his influence and affection in my life. I knew in my mind that if my Grandpa B.C. was here, he would've set some things and people straight about his granddaughter. I imagined how his big heart and big wallet could've been the difference-maker in my life.

The fact is life is what life is, and despite my ability or willingness to acknowledge it, everything that has happened and that is happening is a scene on the stage of my life and a chapter in the book of my life called my Plan A. There is no way that I can factor out every issue that I've encountered and filter my life free of conflict, nor can I interject my fairy tale, knight-in-shining armor, happily-ever-after endings either. It didn't matter how much I longed for a different past; I couldn't change it.

What I didn't know is that every regret, pity party and hypothetical situation that I built in my mind, was keeping me from living in the present and it was keeping me from advancing into the future. I have been applauded by some and snubbed by others for going back to acknowledge and unpack my history of sexual abuse in my last book, *Forgiveness*. Although I owe nobody an explanation for pursuing healing and wholeness, I had no choice, but to do it. I felt like I had come to a decision between sanity or insanity. I had gotten to the end of my rabbit hole and had regained my stature like Alice in Wonderland, the food needed to shrink me to a size to allow me to escape my entrapment was out of my reach.

The only choices I had at that moment were to either breakthrough, be stuck forever, or wait for a rescuer. The little girl that had been downsized, diminished, and ignored, was stuck inside a 40- year-old frame. I made the decision to stop living in a hypothetical life, zeroing out and denying my past and settled down in my soul to accept and repaint my present and my future on a canvas of truth and come to grips with every facet of me.

All the "what ifs," allowed me to hide the idiosyncrasies of who I was and not fully embrace how awesome of a survivor I was. The, "what-ifs," caused me to try to build myself up in the false pretense that I needed to be silent and stoic in order to walk in the shoes of the strong black woman, whatever that means. The "what-ifs," kept me in a scurry to accomplish more so that I could offer the world accolades instead of the totality of who I was. The "what ifs," allowed me to ignore portions of who I was, and the parts that I didn't want included in Sharetta's Plan A. There was no other plan for my life, but in the moment and in my fragmented attempt at coping, I was trying to do life without acknowledging the broken little girl.

The fact of the matter is, in my Plan A, that little girl played an important foundational role. There is no real me without her. Heaven forbid if anyone thought that I was mentally unstable. Even someone joking and saying that I was crazy, stoked an argument. I was trying to be whole by omitting blocks from my life and without admitting that I had issues. Although I wanted to be healed, my faith and my awareness was not activated to see that my disease wasn't incurable if I only acknowledged it. The Savior's hem was available to me then and even now to be healed and made whole.

I know that some things are so cruel, traumatic, and life-altering that many survivors repress memories in order to cope. This chapter isn't making lite of real defense mechanisms. Memory repression often requires another level of healing, acceptance and sometimes even clinical treatment to facilitate healing. I had the memories, vivid memories, but opted to deny the mental effects and attempted to disassociate myself from the turn of events. Purpose is in the pain that you've endured. Purpose is in the pain that I have experienced. The very pain that we are trying to edit out of our past is the breeding ground for purpose.

So, you too can break down your walls and break through the ceiling of your life and understand that there is no Plan B. The hurt, pain, scars, or the lack thereof were known as a part of your Plan A from the foundations of the earth. As a matter of fact, some struggles are necessary for the magnitude of the ministry that you will accomplish in the earth. Nothing catches God by surprise. Despite Him being an amazing God and an awesome Father, bad things still happen to good people and people that we perceive as bad individuals can actually experience blessings.

As long as you search for the plan B and can't accept the tract you're on right now, you will be stagnated. Even if the tract is totally wrong, acknowledge and accept that you must make changes, but you are enough as a person. You may need to solicit help to change the trajectory of your life, but you are still enough. Your worth isn't attached to your accomplishments or present conditions. Self-worth is a matter of the heart. Understand how much has been invested in you to get you to this present moment. Every dart, every fiery attack that came for your life, you overcame. When I have low moments, I think on the work that the Lord has done in me and is continuing to do. I think on His sacrifice that was made for me. Even though, His hand didn't reach from Heaven and manually scoop me up out of my issues, He provided ways of escape and places of refuge for me.

My prayer for you is that you no longer be pressured to be what people want you to be, no longer feel incomplete without their acceptance. A clique, whether it's in church, family, or business, cannot add value to a person who feels valueless when it's time to stand alone. Remove the dimmer switch from your life. Holy Spirit will help you tweak your identity as you go. Shine bright in your own individuality. You were created for undeniable greatness.

Ungodly mentalities become molded if left unchallenged; but God is able to break the mold without destroying the person!

—Apostle Maxine Evans Gray, Jackson, MS

CHAPTER 11

Rock Your Lane

Please understand that you cannot change anything that has happened in your life. I won't try to downplay past hurts, but I will say seek healing quickly. Worrying about your future is just as unproductive as being stuck in the past. The best advice I can give you is to live now. Live in your lane. Paul said in 2 Timothy 4:7, *I have fought the good fight, I have finished my course, I have kept the faith*. His course was his lane in life. His course was his race.

His course was the calling and the work that he was anointed and appointed to complete. Each of us have one. As a youngster, I'm pretty sure that Paul thought that his plight in life was to rid the world of Christians. If you have read anything about Paul, you'll know that he started with a hate for Christians that was evident in his persecution of them. But God got Paul's attention by taking away his physical vision temporarily. When Paul's vision was restored, he also had a newfound spiritual vision.

Just as Paul had a spiritually awakening experience, you may have one too, but if nothing happens that was as dramatic as his experience what will you do? Most of the time epiphanies come when you are in motion. I haven't heard many fearful and stagnant couch potato spiritual awakenings. Get up, dust yourself off, and get in motion. The race starts when the flag drops and the pistol fires.

You must be in position for that start. You can't be at home wondering if you are qualified or equipped.

This is not the time to over-think or self-doubt. You have been called. People are depending on you, but most importantly you are depending on you. You need to see yourself successful in your lane just as much as anyone does. So, what if you make a mistake. The Bible says in Proverbs 24:16 that a just man falls seven times, but he continues to get back up.

The falls aren't the result of a deliberate error, but the result of intentional strides to complete the course, to rock their lane. With every falling experience you get the opportunity to capture and benefit from the lessons and the experiences. You learn how to maneuver better the next time. If you never venture out, you have already written the ending to your story. God is the author and finisher of my life. I really want to see how the course that he set before me plays out.

Over the years, my husband and I have made many attempts at entrepreneurship. We believe in working, but really have a desire to free up some of our time from being confined and restricted to workplace. We have tried multi-level marketing businesses, our own trucking company and even had a restaurant. In hindsight, most of the things that we tried were not really our true lane and eventually we pulled the plug on those things. We knew it then, but we wanted what we wanted. Does that mean we failed? Absolutely not. We are still going.

We learned lessons in loyalty, excellence, timing, discernment and finances. Praise God we are not in debt as a result of any venture we have tried, but we have gained lifelong lessons as a result. We are still going. Aside from our corporate jobs, we are writing books, speaking, and just being present and available to touch lives for the Kingdom of God. Even the writing and ministry is not the pinnacle of what God is going to do in us and through us, but at least we know that we are in the right lane this time.

The problem that most people have with rocking their own lane in life is they hate to start at the ground level and compare their rate of acceleration to other people. Most would love to pass GO and collect $200, but that's the case most of the time. If we experience acceleration, it's usually because we've already started at the water treading stage. Entry level or ground level is not a bad position. It may seem like it when you're out in the field tending sheep like young David was before he became King. He sat there day in and day out guarding animals enduring the stench and protecting them from evil. This may have been a degrading experience especially since his brothers were set apart to train for and participate in war. Ground zero was not David's final destination. David was meticulous about his assignments, protecting sheep from lions and bears. He was meticulous about his gift as minstrel so much so that evil spirits left Saul as David played the harp. He minded his own business and dared not compare his grace to anyone else's. Rocking his lane caused David to be promoted from shepherd boy to the King of Jerusalem. He traded the shepherd's staff for the king's crown. What an amazing transition.

We all have had bottom of the barrel experiences that prepare us to live in purpose, on purpose and in our own lane. Do not despise the day of your small beginnings. The small beginnings are temporary, but your lane and your course are a lifelong journey. The small beginning may be for you, but as you mature and progress, you will see your lane is so much larger than you or your current circumstances. I'm almost certain that there are people needing you to get into position so that you can reach back and help them get into position. God is all-sufficient, but he uses the ministry of people to help bring His plans and purposes into fruition in the earth.

The children of Israel were enslaved for 400 years in Egypt while awaiting the arrival of a deliverer to the scene. We all know that God delivered them, but Moses became the go-between, the person in the gap, the conduit, the channel. You are the same for someone in the earth. You may not be called to everyone, but your lane will Divinely cross paths with other people who you are called to. Everything is not your niche, your business venture, or your course in life.

Most times that connection will be to the advantage of both parties. In Luke 1:41, we see Elizabeth who was pregnant with John the Baptist and Mary who was pregnant with Jesus meet as Mary approaches Elizabeth's house. The anointing and grace that Mary carried caused the baby in Elizabeth to leap. Then Elizabeth called Mary blessed and the mother of her Lord.

The two ladies established a bond, but the connection between the two fetuses didn't stop. John the Baptist paved the way of salvation with his call to repentance. He then Baptized Jesus and prepared Him to go into the wilderness. John also knew his role and his lane. Although he called the people to repentance before Jesus started His ministry, John the Baptist knew the magnitude of Jesus' ministry. John the Baptist knew his course. Instead of becoming indignant and territorial, he said in John 3:30, that he had to decrease his ministry so that the ministry of Jesus could increase.

If we are allowing God to be the author and finisher of our faith and of our stories, we must decrease and allow God-ordained purposes to increase in our lives. Our destiny in life is not just to get college degrees, a career, a home with a white picket fence, spouse, and children, and then retire and die. There is a bigger picture and a greater story with a larger purpose.

We are the body of Christ. We reach out. We touch other's lives. We encourage people with testimonies of our journeys. Believe it or not, it helps to help others. Your lane becomes meaningful and gratifying because you know what it took to get you from emotional and psychological slums to this radiant person that's willing to go behind enemy lines to perform rescue and recovery missions. Helping people to discover their identity, their authenticity, and their purpose.

Outro
Don't Stop Evolving

You will accomplish much as you seek to learn more about yourself and pursue destiny and purpose. You will open and close chapters along the way. Your ultimate goal is to complete your leg of the race in excellence. Completion of your course will happen if you continue to make necessary adjustments in life. Don't stop evolving into the asset to the world that you are becoming. God is a productive and progressive God. Your level of grace should increase. Your knowledge base should increase. Your keenness in the Spirit should increase. In 2 Corinthians 3:18, we see that the more we live and dwell in Christ, we are being transformed more and more from one level of glory to another level of glory. Welcome your transformation.

I'm sure you have heard people brag and confess that they will never change. For me, change is inevitable. There is nothing glorious or profitable about not growing and evolving. We should not only welcome change but expect it. I understand that change and transformation is scary and that could be the reason that we teeter totter between changing and remaining the same, but in submitting to change we may find solutions to the issues that we face in this labyrinth called life.

The fact of the matter is, the progression of our lives will continue chronologically whether we choose to participate in the progression of self-development or not. Take your evolution seriously. Repossess your life from situations and circumstances. You can't be governed by those events. Timing is imperative, but you can't even be controlled by biological clocks. Your timing and seasons should be governed by God's design for your life. Knowing your identity and purpose in the various seasons of your life can be like a synchronized dance. It is beautiful and graceful when the moves are smart, smooth and calculated. Don't be discouraged if a mistake happens. Just keep dancing. Just keep evolving. The more you continue the dance and pursue the Son, the more you will be transformed into the radiant evolution of you.

About the Author

Sharetta Donalson is an admired mentor to women from various walks of life. Her wisdom and advice are birthed through her many life's challenges coupled with the Word of God. She is formally trained in ministry through Growing Upwards Bible School at her home church, New Beginnings Christian Life Center in Ridgeland, MS. She received certification as a Christian Life Coach from P4 Coaching Institute in Rocky Mount, N.C. She has experienced great success as an author in her book, *Forgiveness: The Quest for Healing Your Heart* and has co-authored twice in anthologies for trauma survivors.

She serves in Jackson, MS in her profession as a Registered Nurse. She received her foundational educational at a local community college and eventually attained a bachelor's degree from the University of Phoenix in Phoenix, AZ.

Sharetta is a Canton, Mississippi native and continues to live in Mississippi with her husband, Anderson. They enjoy spending time with their five children and their grandchild.

Contact Information: ForwardSpeaking@gmail.com

Made in the USA
Columbia, SC
31 December 2019